Dave Viney grew up in Stretford, Manchester. He started writing poetry and short stories at the age of 14, largely in secret - due to a shortage of poets in the area and an excess of people who liked to punch poets in the face. He spent the next 19 years doing things that he had no idea would interest a group of staring, expectant strangers, then first set foot on stage in Manchester's Greenroom in summer 2009 for open mic night Freed Up - a night he would later co-host with Dominic Berry.

Host of Bang Said the Gun: Manchester and a regular guest at poetry nights across the UK, he has written and performed for BBC Manchester Radio, written and performed two sell out shows at the Lowry Theatre as part of the Working Verse Collective, was the 2013 Poet Laureate of Kendal Calling Festival and in 2014 debuted his one man spoken word show 'Shapes' at the Edinburgh Fringe.

Dave Viney

A POET CALLED DAVE

Flapjack Press
flapjackpress.co.uk

exploring the synergy between performance and the page

Published in 2015 by Flapjack Press
Salford, Gtr Manchester
flapjackpress.co.uk & @FlapjackPress

ISBN 978-0-9576639-8-5

Author photo on page 1 by Dominic Berry
Illustrations on pages 73 & 74 by Brink
Cover design by the author & Brink
'Waiting for mum' cover photo by Constance Viney
'Waiting to go on' cover photo by Ian Sinkovits

Printed by Lonsdale Direct
Wellingborough, Northants
lonsdaledirect.co.uk

'Hobson's Choice Words' was first published in *Best of Manchester
Poets, vol. 2* [Puppywolf, 2011], 'Kiss My Assets' in *Word Gumbo, vol.
1.1* [Gumbo Press, 2011], 'That Field', 'Dad's Justice', 'The Snides',
'The Proper Bloke's Last Stand', 'The Absent Friend', 'True
Britannia', 'Corporate Punishment', 'My Mind Is Spider-Man', 'A
Game Of Two Scarves' and 'What I Know' in Working Verse
Collective's *The Prequel to the Sequel* [Flapjack Press, 2012], and
'Sonnet To The Cynical' in Bang Said the Gun's *Mud Wrestling
With Words* [Burning Eye, 2013].

This book is dedicated to The *Sound* Society.
I'd be lost in life (and poetry) without you:

To the life-givers, the lifescapers, the manner-makers, the risk-takers, the back-watchers, the lip-lockers, the Dave-definers, the feet-finders, the gig-givers, the put-me-uppers, the ear-lenders, the bin-drinkers (not a typo), the trick-teachers, the party-starters, the mind-benders, the mind-menders, the truth-talkers and the heart-holders.

To the Bang Gang: Daniel Cockrill, Martin Galton, Peter Hayhoe, Rob Auton, Laurie Bolger, Jack Rooke, Sarah Redington - for the warm welcome whatever the season.

To the Stretford Seven (in order of appearance): Pat Mulrooney, Scott Caplan, Steven Vaughan, Aidy Franks, Tim Nichol, Chris Nichol, Stuart McPhee - without all of whom the adventure would have been lacking. Mancs for the memories.

To (the ever supportive, awe inspiring) Claire, Maggie, Brian, Joe, Margy, Graham, Emma and Co. - whose belief never wavered, even when mine did. I won the loved ones Lottery with you lot.

To Brink, friend and Editor.

To Steven Patrick Morrissey and Johnny Marr for writing the soundtrack.

Cheers all.

What a ride!

Contents

Poetry has a bad reputation: cravat wearing introspective oddballs who don't know what Poundland is or how much everything costs there, people who write using the pointy end of a feather... However, Dave Viney is fighting this bad rep just by existing. He's one of those people who get asked if they're going to court whenever they've got a suit on; he deffo knows what Poundland is and how much things cost there and he's not happy about it. I imagine at some point in his life he has probably got a cob on with a feather, and I'm guessing he writes with one of them pens you can nick from Argos.

Honest, droll, narky and genuinely funny with stand-out lines that stick in your head - he is the opposite of a CBeebies presenter. Aggressively unpretentious but with a real love of language. Catch him in real life if you can.

Jackie Hagan

Know many poets called Dave? Apart from me obviously.

Thought not.

And yet supposedly everyone knows one. A Dave that is, not a poet. Some say it's a risky strategy being a Dave. Will you be taken seriously? After all, there's a whole comedy channel named after you. Your name is a punchline in almost every episode of *Only Fools and Horses*. Will you endear yourself to working men's clubs, but not performance venues? Will you rue being you? Dave is debatable: would David Bowie have been so successful if he was called *Dave* Bowie? We'll never know. I could have been a ~~contender~~ David, but I find that the name David reminds me of being in trouble with either my mum, my dad, my teachers, or the police in my early teens (I was more wrong crowd, wrong time, wrong place than wrongun.) It's too formal. In fact, I sometimes tense up when I'm called David by someone who doesn't know me well enough to know that it's Dave, or Viney (most people call me Viney), because when I was a lot younger than I am now the name *David* meant *Make yourself scarce*.

It's pronounced 'Vine-ee' by the way. I've had all sorts of mispronunciations, misnames and misnomers. I think the worst was probably 'Vinyl' - Dave Vinyl - it's like the name of the world's worst DJ. As if the name *Dave* isn't '80s enough!

I've been introduced on stage as many things, including "Stretford's finest" (if only that was a compliment), "The Karl Pilkington of Poetry" (which I think was intended to imply dry wit, but could also have been an insult), "The Bastard Child of Carol Ann Duffy and Ross Kemp" (which I can only apologise wholeheartedly to them for), and "Poetry's answer to the question people didn't know to ask" (which I think is quite clever and alludes to my minimal marketing strategy at the time, or being skint as some people like to call it).

I'm joking about Stretford by the way. I love the place. I probably shouldn't do - it's a teacher of tough lessons - but you have to, don't you. The place where you come from *is* you. In part anyway. And it features a lot on these pages in one way or another.

The first poem I ever wrote (and still the most succinct) was called 'Sticks & Stones':

Sticks & Stones

In the back of the riot van
tension ran riot.

I didn't know it was a poem at the time. I just knew that I liked the play on words and making light of dark situations.

I would have to put the reason that I started *performing* poetry down to the first two poetry gigs that I saw. I was extremely lucky: the first (at Manchester's Royal Exchange Theatre) was Lemn Sissay, Henry Normal and Johnny Dangerously (John Bramwell, who would later go on to form the excellent Manchester band 'I am Kloot'). It really opened my eyes as to what poetry could be - relevant, resonating, funny and (to me, at least) cool.

The second was the late and great Hovis Presley at Manchester's Greenroom. Hovis was nothing like I thought a poet would be. Nothing like I thought a poet *could* be. I didn't know this kind of thing was allowed - this level of dry humour and (to some degree) vulnerability, from a bloke! An actual bloke. Because to all intents and purposes that's what Hovis was - a really nice, humble, funny bloke who could do poetry. The image of long haired lotharios, wearing velvet smoking jackets and reading from parchment was smashed to pieces forever that night.

Those two gigs sowed the seed. But it wouldn't be until nearly 13 years later, in October 2009, that I would perform a poem for the first time (in the same space that Hovis had) at the Greenroom. It took me 13 years to believe that I could say anything worth hearing. I can still remember the paper shaking in my hand, and the poets who would later become great friends, telling me that I should come back. My only regret is not doing it sooner.

In poetry terms I'm still a baby, and yet over the last five years I've had the pleasure of seeing new talent emerge almost every year. If the buzz around poetry continues at its current pace, this could end up being the fastest growing spokenword scene since the Beat Poets of the late fifties. Obviously it could fizzle out, too. But thanks to YouTube, people are breaking through much faster than they would have in the past. If you're a performance poet starting out, you have never had a better time than right now to get on a stage and show people what you can do. Poetry is in danger of becoming popular. Act accordingly.

Personally (and publically, I suppose) I've had the pleasure of meeting some amazing people and artists (in that order) and performing in some great places, but in early 2013 I was diagnosed with a condition called BDD (Body Dysmorphic Disorder), which can manifest itself in a number of different ways and different intensities within different people. In me, it manifests itself by convincing my mind that if I don't follow a healthy, balanced diet and exercise regime then my body shape, complexion, facial lines, facial shape - even teeth - are all susceptible to change within an hour of it crossing my mind. I know this is impossible. But it is so vivid that I have found myself convinced at times that it's real.

It's a cousin of Anorexia and it also seems to feed off nerves, so for a time there I thought I would never set foot on a stage again. I withdrew into myself. I took down all the YouTube footage of me that I could and destroyed it, because I couldn't stomach looking at it.

Now I've learned to manage the condition with the help of counselling, applied logic and the support of friends and family. Plus the kind words and openness of a well-known poet who shall remain nameless, but worked through the same condition himself and is a top bloke to boot. Cheers mate. If anything, the experience of BDD has made me more determined to give my all on stage and beat the bastard back. Let the rebuilding of my YouTube footage commence! The term *My own worst critic* has never felt so apt.

Thank you for buying this book. I really appreciate it and I hope you enjoy reading it as much as I've enjoyed writing and performing it. Some of my non-poetry friends have asked in the past how to read poetry. Personally, I read it like a normal book - no pregnant pauses at the end of each line, I just read it and imagine a rhythm. I always try to write with a rhythm in mind. To split this book into sections, I shared the material with people who aren't shy of an opinion and quoted their reactions.

WARNING FOR THE EASILY OFFENDED: there is some swearing in this book. Leaving out profanities which are used in everyday language feels like a cop out and an unnecessary censorship to me, and although I don't litter my text with expletives I do use them when I think they ring true to the subject and / or the situation.

Also...

When I'm writing about myself as a child, as a teenager, or a man (ahem, no jokes please), I try to recall my mannerisms, thoughts, phraseology and any speech patterns from the time in question, in order to try and bring an authentic feel to the poem. With that in mind, you may notice slight changes in style and tone throughout the book. This is intentional. I don't know if I have an overall 'style' - I just write it how I feel it at the time.

Lastly...

Please feel free to say hello if we're at the same event (and you want to). I don't know if I look like an approachable person (probably not), but I am and one who's potentially on his own in your strange town ☺. Also, feel free to befriend me on Facebook or follow me on Twitter (@vineypoet). But don't follow me in the street. I will probably call the police. You know who you are. Respect the Restraining Order.

Ta and ta-ra,

Viney xx

We, The Poets

We, the poets
will not know our limits,
will not give failure a second thought,
or a third,
or a fourth,
will not apologise for poetry as an art form.
We will start a brainstorm in a teacup
and though we may only end up
with a hurricane in a kettle,
we will still romanticise our meteoric rise
to obscurity.
We will climb like photosynthesised high rises
into blinding light,
we will prise open our sleep deprived eyes
just to alphabeticalize our lives,
beginning with the word
Affected
and ending with the word
Zombie.

We, the poets
will encourage life
to rub us up the wrong way,
so that we can write the right way.
We will not *grow out of it,*
we will not *get a hold of ourselves,*
will not melt away into middle-age mediocrity.
We will go when we're good(ish) and ready.

We will age like a fine line crossed on a regular basis.
Our faces will become poems for poets,
whose faces will become poems for poets,
whose faces will become poems for poets

and we will hold up our hang ups
and wring them out for you like dishcloths.

Dirty,
irrational
dishcloths.

We, the poets
will not go quietly,
will not pass politely
into a TV evangelist's pearly white afterlife,
because there's nothing there for us.
It's not dysfunctional enough.
Leave your spark at the gate
by the sign that says
HEAVEN:
ALL PERKS.
NO QUIRKS.

And you can say "Heaven is whatever you want it to be."
But we've seen it on TV - it's all dry ice and white suits,
a who's who of "Who let you in?
Did no-one tell you it's no tattoos?
Oh my god! Are those Scars? Is that self-harm?
Security! ...*Security!*"

We, the poets
will keep believing
that we must be doing something right,
because sometimes,
you look like you might be *listening*,
like you may think that what we're saying's interesting?
Or not. You lot could just be great liars
and if so we, the poets
admire your flare for descriptive dishonesty.

I, the poet
(one man; of minor significance
in the grand scheme of things)
am wary of saying *We, the poets* too many times.
You see, I don't want your enduring memory of this poem,
or this book for that matter,
to be that it grated,
and so with that in mind
I dedicate both to you
in the hope that a lickle tickle of your ego
will do the trick
(the one where you saw me in half
and I wiggle my toes -
I like that one).

Thank you.

"SOMETHING THAT REMINDS YOU OF OUR CHILDHOOD?"

Dave Viney
(Voted 'Best Big Brother' in a poll
of one completely impartial older brother)

"RUSTY SCAFFOLDING AND ROTTING TIMBER - PLACES WE WEREN'T SUPPOSED TO BE."

Joe Viney
(Younger brother and co-conspirator)

That Field

That field
(opposite the Freedman's,
next to the Mulrooney's)
was more than a field to me.

That field -
just grass to the untrained eye.
A wasteland for wasting time
that would later be cherished,
but it was more than a field to me.

That field
was a battlefield
littered with the limbs
of out-of-favour action figures
and the odd marble.

That field
destroyed evidence for us -
mopped up our blood, our sweat
and our tears,
and all before teatime.
Complicit in our petty crimes.
Would definitely have winked if it could.

That field's gone now.
Our memories swept up
with a pneumatic dustpan and brush,
dumped in a landfill
with eras past their sell-by date
and second-hand childhoods.

Replaced
by *New-builds*.

New people who have no time
for old time's sake.

Every now and then,
when I walk past those houses,
I imagine an epic action figure battle
raging in their foundations:
a rag-tag band of amputee, dog-eared heroes,
against a horde of weather-worn, torn apart tyrants.

And I think how great it would be
if in a thousand years time
when sifting through the rubble,
an archaeologist says the words...

"And what we have here is a splendid example
of the Pre New-build Thundercats Period."

Dad's Justice

Summer 1985
and a look that we knew only too well -
behind dad's eyes
Wanted posters were going up:

BIKE THIEVES WANTED
DEAD OR DEAD

To hear mum tell it,
our house was the last bastion of home security:
fences too rickety to climb,
weeds fashioned into trip wires
and a cat with anger management issues
on 24 hour purrtrol.
She never mentions the attention seeking
Pick me! padlock on the shed.

Then there was the window sticker -
pure sticky-back lies
for the thickest of thieves:

WARNING - THIS HOUSE IS ALARMED.

Yeah, ok mum - if you say so.
Tell it to our telly,
'cause the space where the video used to be
ain't listenin'!

Dad could maintain evil eye contact
all the way through the winding down of a car window -
a skill that we were completely in awe of.
Could tame name-makers,
steel toe-capped ball breakers -

lads that sweated warm beer,
fags and fighting.
Chests deflated, shoulders sagged,
cheek in check.

But it stayed Bike Thieves 1 Vigilante Dads 0
and we adapted to pedestrian adventures,
but dad never got his justice.

In June the following year,
the pageant came to Stretford:

kids with candyfloss,
kids with balloons,
kids with BIKES.

Every cyclist a suspect.

Every bike a lookalike.

Clunk click - every trip.
Best advice I never had,
flying down the motorway with a kamikaze dad.
And I should've made a mix-tape
that said 'I'm my father's son!',
but I made Crimes Against Music
by Stock, Aitken & Waterman

because I have no idea what you like.

You're a *days out dad* now,
a Random Radio Man
and the dial always goes
to any band I've never heard of,
but I am mad keen to know
just one song,
so we can talk about it,
so we can *laugh* about it.

I'm Ball at his feet Happy Boy,
but I haven't got the skills
to know how the gaps in conversations
are adequately filled,
so I sit tight-lipped in this passenger seat,
perfecting my forward stare
and yes, I'm aware of the popular saying
about a problem shared,
but even when I'm older
I might still not have the balls
to ask you the whys or what ifs
in case you gave me what for.

And now the memory of the night we left

gets louder in this silence,
when mum snuck in and got us dressed
in the middle of the night
and she made us play a game where we were quiet...
(smart my mum)
and you asleep with no idea
of the damage that you'd done.
And our Joe, well... he was just a baby
and then no-one really *talked* for ages
and now I've got nothing, but loads to say and...

Dad, I just want to say this trip's been amazing
and you're not the 15 foot, evil-eyed
smacking-machine I remember.

But I can't say that to you, because it's you
and 'cause you might use it against mum.
"Just here on the corner'll do.

Nice one."

Wacky Woodchip

Partially de-chipped woodchip wallpaper
goes bump in the night.
Seemingly seamless cobbled walls
refracting moonlight.

It's a boxroom pox,
a pebbledashed trap,
a cell made entirely from bubble wrap,
a dotty dichotomy
on a mind-boggling scale.

Teenage angst
spelt out in braille.

I only glance up for a second.
A glance becomes a zombie stare.
I thought escape was possible,
but mum says her wallpaper is
"Going nowhere!"

My eyes are bloodshot,
my language X-Rated.

The doctor says my illness is

woodchip related.

The Snides

They crouch.
Each fast Baltic breath
faster than the last fast Baltic breath.
Hugging the red bricks beneath that kitchen window
like two piss poor Spider-Man impersonators
(with no power comes no point finishing that sentence, really).
Manchester in December.
Not the weather for a mission like this;
threatens to give away their position with
smoke signal breath -
breath that spells out i n t r u d e r s
when the truth is...
complicated.

What do you do when you're caught
between a court case and a kicking?
Between a rock and a Rockport?
In short - good kids in bad company.

The kitchen light comes on!
Not your modern day *slow glow, eco friendly,*
energy saving kitchen light.
This is a *sting the eyes, meter munching, carbon footprint,*
no tint - in your face! 1989 kitchen light,
and they panic!

Eyes: clanging alarm bells, hit with hammer hearts,
thought bubbles filled with exclamation marks -
no-one has ever been more scared than they are right now!

I know this, because one of them is me.

In the shadows by the front gate,
The Snides urge us silently on to their prize

and we start
        stutter
   stop
           rise
like the grabber on the crane arm at the fair,
but Snides don't fish for teddy bears -
their prize is a black leather handbag
on the kitchen counter.
Our prize:
getting home...
nothing bruised,
nothing broken.

We look at each other.
He looks at the garden fence,
then back at me
to see if I got what he meant...
If I run, will you run?

For a second
I worry that my look to him said
I want my mum!

But then we're running.

Not a present day me *listening for creaks,*
muscle tweaks and praise the lord for hot baths kind of run.
Me at fourteen - *immaculate hamstrings,*
spring-heeled and knees like precision engineering.

The kind of run that's so confident in its own ability,
you can stop mid-stride and shout "Fuck you!"
Ok, so maybe not *that* confident.
But it's the kind of run
that over the coming months,
we'd better get used to.

The Snides (Part 2)

Freeze frame on our laughing faces;
the film adaptation
of an Enid Blyton book,
set in Manchester in the late 1980s.
But that wasn't us.
Our beating was waiting in the wings
for that scene to end, like it always was.

In Chapter One of *our* book,
we'd make the distinction between the Snides
and the fictional slick back six-pack bad guys,
glamorised in films around that time.
Trust me, Snides are more varied on the outside
and much darker on the inside.
And there were no larger than life,
pinstriped slapstick gangsters either.
No singing, no dancing.
Not on my street anyway.

*"We could've been anything that we wanted to be -
yes the decision was ours."*

Thank you Bugsy Malone.
But we couldn't
and it wasn't.

They made us *pick 'n' nick* kids,
hated our innocence,
played us like idiots,
and though we were smarter than them
we felt like boys and they seemed like men,
so we *became* idiots for them.

Chapter Two

It just hangs there doesn't it;
that mix of tension and fear -
never really mentioned is it,
never put into words.
It can be heard though sometimes,
muffled through coat linings
when they're rolling and wrestling,
when coats get pulled up hard over faces,
bare-chested, cold-fisted blows on ribcages
and yeah you know not to respect it,
but you can't disrespect it either,
so you flatter to deceive it -
act like you're in awe of it.
Lie *for* it, never *to* it.
Well alright, sometimes to it,
but only if you have to,
because you know what happens if it catches you out
and you never tell an adult,
because the truth is too brutal for them, too ugly,
too mug me and call it 'Taxing',
too tragic,
too graphic,
too halfway through a friendly conversation
head-butt.
They're too far-sighted to fear,
too *not round here.*
It's too much -
too school of hard knocks
that makes Grange Hill look like Cambridge.
You're too hollow for any hug to fix.
They're too out of the picture to picture this.
It's too ugly,
too *hug me if you want to,*
but for fuck's sake, will you please just ground me!

You see, round our way
parents get suspicious if you stay in too long -
want to know what's going on
and we all know that after that it's never too long
before that cringey chat about your feelings,
so you roll out a halfway believable
"Nothing mum, I'm fine, honest."
Then you promise.
Then you promise again.
But you know that in a few hours
you'll be back on it, back in it,
back out there with them.

Boys acting like idiots
for boys acting like men.

The Process

Sometimes I find that I'm winging it;
pidgin-English thinking;
links that don't link to anything of substance.
An abundance of options,
but they're lost in translation and trading insults.
The *Old School Ideas* baulk
"It's not our fault, it's these *Foreign Notions*
poking their nose in;
coming over here,
taking our thoughts!"
To which the *Foreign Notions* retort
"Hey, we're just here working on the ideas
that you think are beneath you
and we cost a lot less in stress per hour than you do."

It's usually around this time
that *Lazy Rhymes* stick their oar in:
"Will you two pack it in, please!
Listen to this. It's the bee's knees.
It's about that guy in the shirt and tie
we saw eating a pie in that lay-by."

We cutaway to *Artistic Integrity*,
who with a wry smile says
"There was no guy.
There were no pies.
You're just rhyming for rhyming's sake
and you should know by now that I'm wise
to it."

Now, I've known it to go on all day like that,
but I have to keep control of the art I chose,
so I change tack -

book-bind loose thoughts into paperbacks,
use creative sparks to light the pages
and stand back.
I don't usually condone an internal book burning,
but my internal waste paper basket is full to the brim
and now the flames climb higher, licking my lips,
shaping the words, SHOUTING the words -

"This IS a dictatorship!

All thoughts will fall in line
or be confined to the *Cabinet of Doom*."
That's the filing cabinet
hidden away in my back bedroom,
where ideas go to die.
The Revolution will not be vocalised.

All wayward thought processes
relent and comply,
except one...

Nostalgia wants one more for the road,
slurs teenage tales of off-the-rails adventure.
Stoically (it's never "woe is me")
recounts the then
in a *Now I've got my hooks in you* kind of way
that reels me in.
Says...

"When I was 13, I got these almost new trainers.
Some other kid's hated gift hand-me-down.
They weren't a cool make, but they made me *feel* cool.
We would hang around in a gang of six or seven.
We didn't have rules as such,
but we did try to spend as much time as possible
in places we weren't supposed to be.

This one time,
we climbed the scaffolding of an old building
and lay there sunbathing with our tops off
(like we would get anything other
than sunburnt and told off),
but we knew best - t-shirts cushioning our heads,
legs dangling off that roof like we were glued to it.

Half an hour in, sun blazing and us brazenly ignoring
every parental nugget we'd ever been given,
we hear this...
'David!... David!... DAVID!'
I'm thirteen.
I am painfully aware that adding an 'id' to my name
can mean only one thing.
I'm in for it, man. Big time!
And so we're all sign language and whispered swear words.
I compare worst case scenarios,
that all start with a *Why me?*,
because we all know who that voice belongs to,
but it can't be.
We told no-one where we were going,
so there's no way she could know.
How could she?

It's 24 degrees.
But we lie there frozen.
For a moment we harbour the naïve hope
that she's gone home...
and then we hear it.
'David! Get down here now! I know it's you.
I can see your trainers.'

It's hard to explain how I feel in that moment,
because knowing you've made a schoolboy error,

combined with the abject terror of a raging mum
is not a feeling you savour."

Nostalgia knows I'm on the ropes.
Brings out a Heavyweight to deliver that knockout blow.
From a cloud of theatrical smoke,
ducking and diving...
Poignancy makes its way to the ring,
to a musical medley
of every song that's ever moved me.
Stands toe to toe,
looks at me all doe-eyed and says

"I don't know if you know this...
Your mum trades on that story, too.
But in the version *she* tells people

your trainers are new."

Handle With Care

If I'm honest,
my first thought was a box holding fragile belongings.
An image more palatable, more manageable.
Damageable, but wrapped in bubble-wrap
and cushioned against blows.
No such luxury afforded
to the uninsured minds of children.
To them it's not about being popular.
Their outlook is visceral.
Popular is pop star impossible.
Popular is sleep-overs and school trips
when someone sits next to you.
Popular is being picked for the team,
before the only one left is you.
Popular is for popular people.

We see only what he shows us
and he shows us very little,
because the only truth he knows
is that grown up truth is fickle
and it will not set *him* free.
You see, to him we seem incapable -
we'll shake up all his valuables,
unable to contain ourselves,
when the label clearly tells us we should

HANDLE WITH CARE.

The box drops
and your treasured possessions,
measured in memories and magnitude,
in mothballs and marriages,

fall to the floor and the damage is insured
but irreparable;
an unbearable truth to you,
but a beautiful truth to her.
Because for her to have the memories and the magnitude,
the mothballs and the marriages,
means that she got through this.
She grew strong enough, long enough to do this
and though she carried her bruises on the inside,
she survived and lived her life in the realisation
that the traits she was told were negative as a child
are positively golden as an adult.

HANDLE WITH CARE.

Beware,
some mums are warriors -
linear and never to be crossed.
Lost temper, tempered to perfection
with an inflection that whispers in your ear
whilst chewing it off.
Know that a lioness protects her cubs with smarts,
not just claws,
and because my mum had a switchblade sweetheart overture,
that was the way she operated;
measured malice;
a balance of polite insistence and threat,
of nice appearance and yet
whatever she said to that kid
made his eyes widen
and he never said a bad word to me again.

HANDLE WITH CARE.

Show them that shyness can be humility,
that standing alone is strength, not vulnerability,

that one day their detractors will yearn to be different
in *any* way,
that they are magnificent and that, on a daily basis,
you find your strength in them,
that their quirks are charisma,
that their character is bigger than the burden of words,
that they will become the most gloriously complex,
inspirational people in the world,
that between them and you, every problem has a solution
and that you are just one of the most imperfect people
they'll ever be introduced to.
Tell them they'll never deserve to be attacked
and remember to say
"I will always have your back.

Always."

"ONE SMALL STEP FOR MAN. ONE GIANT LEAP FOR LADKIND."

Brian Viney
(Father and emergency rescue from anywhere
at any time *in twenty minutes*)

Lad 1:
"I'm in therapy.
Basically, I'm building a house.
Not a house in the traditional sense -
A house made with achievements instead of bricks,
with hope instead of mortar,
and in order to allow the inner me to flourish unrestricted
there will be no roof on this house, nothing at all."

Lad 2:
"So you're building a wall?"

Lad 1:
"No, it's not a wall.
It's a condominium of contentment
and it will have a pool that isn't actually a pool.
It's a bottomless well of opportunity."

Lad 2:
"Right. I see.
So is it a pool or a well?"

Lad 1:
"Well it's technically a pool.
But it's also a metaphorical well,
and if I were to lower a metaphorical bucket into it
it would potentially come back up
with some metaphorical opportunities in it.
Can you not get me in a headlock please?!?
It's making it very hard to focus on my safe place."

The Proper Bloke's Last Stand

Why are you here?
This is a Poetry Slam.
Maybe you thought it was a metaphor
for cage-fighting bards.

I begin at a disadvantage -
you have already started the clock
on your 60 second building project.

Yeah, you smile,
but behind those eyes
a team of eager realists
quick-brick a wall to keep out
malfunctioning words,

busy with trowels and mortar -
a mixer, two parts disinterest,
four parts discomfort,
spinning behind them.

You call a break, down tools…
"Hold up lads…
This one seems like a *proper* bloke -
watches football,
plays football,
likes a pint and grew up
on the same streets we did -
thick-skinned and thankful
for the shrewd eyes
in the back of his bruised head."

"But he ponces about with words boss -
moulds 'em into fancy rhymes,

puts lipstick on 'em
and asks 'em to whisper in our ears -
makes 'em sound less... *Blokey.*
Words should be A to Z,
A to B,
B&Q!"

Work resumes
and I try to throw a nostalgia-shaped spanner
into your works, but it's too late -
the wall is finished.
Your attention has called it a day.

Sounding not quite as *Blokey* as I'd like,
I attempt to salvage something of our
performer / audience relationship...

"Look, I wouldn't usually do this.
But if it would put you at ease,
I could punch you in the face?"

The Absent Friend

There's a part of that lad
that will always have that
same old Berghaus jacket on,
that will always be the one who's
on one,
and the heart on that lad!
Bigger than the biggest kind-hearted whale's,
smaller than Stretford Arndale,
but only marginally.

There's a part of that lad
that will always be short-hand banter,
the booze-fuelled, sleep-deprived rant,
and the spirit of that lad!
Bigger than the trouble that he sailed through,
better for the pickles he got into...
especially after a jar or two,

or six.

Florida.
Was it something we said?

You were the Pied Piper of the Pie-eyed,
the first to the bar and the last to bed.
Adventure stalked you,
had you in its sights at all times.

Now you're oranges from the Sunshine State
and we're...

clementines from Tesco.

How did that happen?

There's a part of that lad
that will always like rain,

that will always crave
the in-from-the-cold, pint-waiting,
piss-taking certainty
of mates.

And there's a part of me
that still sees that lad 17 and *buzzing!*

Saturday night * Nervous excitement * The Smiths on tape
Ready when he's ready * Downstairs * Parents talking
Mates squirming * Sat down * Coming up
Trying their hardest to act like humans.

"SARCASM AND COMPLAINING.
AT THE SAME TIME. VERY BRITISH."

Maggie Viney
(Mother and 1986 Crazy Crease Ironing Champion)

Dear Brian,

Thank you for your generic, one size fits all email. I decided to reply by letter rather than email as letter writing is a dying art, much like customer service.

By now I expect you are a crack shot with a scrunched up letter of complaint, able to hit a waste paper bin from 20 feet away and that your recycling policy exists solely for the purpose of recycling complaints letters into those teeny tiny single sheets of toilet paper for your teeny tiny train toilets.

Obviously I do not include your disabled toilets in that criticism, as they are actually quite 'roomy' and I enjoy the anticipation as the automated door slides slowly open, similar to the way they revealed the star prize on popular '80s quiz show *Bullseye*:

"And Bully's Star Prize is... A 72 year old woman who didn't understand the locking mechanism, hastily pulling up her Granny Pants! Super, smashing... great."

But I am not just complaining. I am appealing to the side of you that longs for change. I know about the nightmare, Brian. The one that plagues you night after night. The one where you're sat on a packed Northern Rail Train and your name badge that says BRIAN REID - NORTHERN RAIL CUSTOMER SERVICE ADVISOR falls out of your pocket in full view of the passengers, who descend on you with murder in their eyes and tear you limb from limb. But it doesn't have to be that way Bri. This is our chance to change things.

It occurred to me that with winter bearing down on us, you will soon be without your stock excuse of 'leaves on the line'. With this in mind I have come up with some alternative excuses to explain away your daily shortcomings:

> "We are sorry that the 7.29 Northern Rail Service to Liverpool Lime Street is delayed by approximately 45 minutes. This is because the driver had 'bed-hair' and could not wet down his hideous cow-lick for love nor money."

> "We are sorry that the 10.20 Northern Rail service to Hebdon Bridge is delayed by approximately 25 minutes. This is due to a pigeon shaking its head and staring at the driver in a manner that he considered to be *ominous*."

> "We are sorry that the 8.15 Northern Rail service to Manchester Oxford Road has been delayed by approximately 60 years. This is due to the fitting of a flux capacitor in error, causing the train to tear a hole in the time / space continuum and travel back to 1955, where the driver was forced to encourage his future father to have sexual relations with his future mother in order to ensure his own existence."

I require no reward or recognition for these suggestions. Consider them a gift.

I have heard it said that putting on extra carriages isn't rocket science, but obviously it IS rocket science, otherwise you would, and I just want you to know that when I am packed into a carriage with so little space that the overhead luggage racks are starting to look appealing, fighting off a panic attack whilst nuzzling my face into a fat man's armpit, I take some comfort in the knowledge that you have a team of NASA Engineers working through the night to find a solution.

In the interim you could possibly deploy a fine mist of Fabreeze as passengers board the train, ensuring that although they are *packed in* like sardines, they *smell* like a Scandinavian pine forest.

I realise that for the majority of this letter I have focused on the negative aspects of your service. I would however like to compliment you on the use of miserable semi-retired coach drivers for your replacement bus service. Due to the 'Grunt' system that they have in place, whereby they just grunt and require neither a ticket nor a reply, this service has provided a very welcome method of free transport for both myself and a large section of Manchester's inebriated and largely incoherent weekend crowd. Not to mention a nice change of scenery for several members of the homeless community.

I think I will leave it at that for now Brian, as I am working on a life size papier-mâché model of a pensioner (made entirely from the obituary section of newspapers) that I plan to send to the CEO of British Gas. But I look forward to forming a customer service Dream Team with you through the many letters that I have yet to send.

Kindest regards,

Viney xx

The queue for the Customer Disservice desk
takes me by unsurprise -
"Would you mind completing a customer satisfaction survey
while you wait to be dissatisfied?"

Silently practicing a complaints speech so dynamic
it could make the shop assistant
take a soul-searching sabbatical to Tibet -
Seven months training in *Basic Human Interaction,*
a further two months in *Common Courtesy*
and one week in *How to use a biro*
without getting ink all over your hands.

This is the complaints speech to end all complaints speeches -
A *perfect pauses,*
SHOUTS *in all the right places,*
righteous riot act of a speech;
a *left to my own devices,*
and with the benefit of hindsight,
I too might have had a dream kind of speech.
But then the hypnotic voice of British sensibilities kicks in:

"Three, two, one and you're under...
As the queue diminishes so will your resolve.
You will accept the shop assistant's feeble excuses
and a voucher that does not represent
the time that you will never get back
and you will thank her for the privilege.
If you attempt to go against your ingrained,
mustn't cause a fuss Britishness
I *will* make you buy an onion from the Food Court
and eat it, thinking it's an apple.

Now, leave quietly and don't forget to smile."

Nothing About Today Has Been Poetic

This morning, breakfast was just breakfast.
The toast wasn't burnt like the oily black of a desert night.
It wasn't undercooked like a metaphor
for my half-baked ideas.
It didn't display a likeness to Jesus,
like some deity-infused wholemeal imitation
of the Turin Shroud.
It was just toast.

The eggs
(usually a source of multiple poetic possibilities)
must have been egg-napped
and replaced with one dimensional eggs,
laid by a hen with no imagination.
They just sat there

like eggs.

The bus ride to work was equally bad.
Tainted by generic, tight-lipped pensioners
and peripheral but non-descript school children.
Even the driver was standard fare.

Work teetered on terrible,
leaned towards lethargic,
then settled on 'samey'.
There was a moment
when Mike opened his lunchbox
and the way he'd arranged his apple,
chocolate bar and sandwich
made me think of an apple,
a chocolate bar
and a sandwich.

When I arrived home, the cat
(in an act of pure selfishness)
steered well clear of the mat,
preferring instead
to prey on my weakness for furry beggars.

Nothing about cat food is poetic.

The television schedule promised
'thought-provoking drama',
but the only thought it provoked was
I wonder when this thought will happen?

Bedtime arrived like bedtime.
My bed
(once a Coliseum of the Cognitive,
staging battles of the Bulb -
fights to the death
between Ideas and Eyebags)
was just a box-sprung mattress
in an iron frame.
I climbed into bed
like someone climbing into bed
and my head hit the pillow like... ... ...

Hobson's Choice Words

Noisy neighbours,
this is your time!

Go forth and multiply the beat
with 50 inch sub-woofers and tweeters.
Masterbeaters of the highest order,
revel in your disorder.

Give us this day our daily bass
and forgive us our wall-hangings,
as we forgive those who wall bang against us.

Noisy neighbours,
this is your moment!

Assemble your fellow scrotes and vote chaos.

Save us from temptation to sleep
and deliver us from peaceful,
with karaoke / off-key.

But know this...
Our time is coming

and you will not hear us coming,
because we are bleary-eyed black belts in consideration,
a tip-toenado,
a subtle shift in power
and we're raising glass after glass,
hour upon hour

to Payback!

To bitter sweet revenge,
to turning speakers up against the wall at 6.00 a.m.,
with the way-too-loud, dulcet tones of Radio 4 -
like fingernails on blackboards
to the muppets next door.

To the look that says
If I don't sleep tonight,
you might just sleep forever,
to domestics drowned out
by the great British weather,
to the blown fuses, the refuges
and the six week cruises,
to decent breeding, silent reading
and legal proceedings.

We do not wish you dead, although...
the irony would not be wasted on us
if you overdosed on sleeping pills,
or got hit by a truck transporting earplugs.

We'll leave you with this...
Five minutes of peace.
Five whole minutes of peace.

But we'll lace every second,
with the threat of noise
and share a private joke
at your glimmer of hope,
when we offer you Hobson's Choice.

Corporate Punishment

You don't have to be mad to work here,
but it helps if you have a hankering
for mind-blowing boredom
and a manageable drink problem.

He assesses his staff in laughter levels,
looks favourably upon those who crease up
at his Christmas cracker jokes.
Guffaw if you wanna get on.

Dresses to emphasise the gut,
plays limited mobility Top Trumps:
  Orthopaedic Office Chair
  • Seat Height: 565mm
  • Padded Neck-Rest: 8 points
  • Independent Adjustment Levers: 4
but demonstrates the kind of stealth,
over-the-shoulder email reading skills
that can only be learnt
from ninja-themed corporate away-days.

Has a barely visible Hitler moustache
that can be glimpsed peripherally in moments of pure evil.

He's a grade-ist, racist, sadist,
bassist in a Blues band
and he doesn't get the irony!

When he was fifteen, he dumped his girlfriend
using Love Heart Sweets,
because texting hadn't been invented yet.

Some twats make a full recovery,
but once a wanker, always a wanker.
A wanker is as a wanker does
and he does wanker *really well*.

What kind of man
makes a habit of walking through doors
that people hold open
and not saying thank you?

What kind of man
complains about his phone signal
at a funeral?

What kind of man tells you that if he could,
he'd splice the split second subliminal image of cock
into a nun's induction video?

What kind of man
grabs the face of a teenage intern
and pretends to read their acne like braille?

At home in front of his computer;
face lit demonically,
secretary porn minimised,
evil glinting in his eyes -
he works on that big idea
to maximise his staffs' efficiency
and make him rich beyond his mildest dreams:

The Stapler-Holster.

The Photo-Coffee-er.

The Office Chair Commode.

The alarm that *no-one* can sleep through.

But his staff - they're having nightmares.
They're talking in their sleep;
repeating after me...
"You don't have to be mad to work here,
but it helps."
"You don't have to be mad to work here,
but it helps."
"You don't have to be mad to work here,
but it helps if you have very limited options."

After receiving a balance-busting gas bill

Channel ANGER

4.15 GAS IN THE ATTIC
Gloria Hunniford scours the attics of Britain in search of propane gas canisters, which (thanks to rising fuel prices) are now more valuable than Grand Papa's 18th Century, diamond encrusted pocket watch.

4.45 GAS WARS
Episode IV, A NEW BILL. It is a period of civil war. Rebel Pensioners, striking from a hidden base (Marjorie's House), have won their first victory against the evil Energy Empire. During the battle, rebel spies managed to steal secret plans to the Empire's ultimate weapon (the COLD SPELL) - a weather phenomenon with enough power to destroy an entire monthly budget. Pursued by the Emperor's sinister bailiffs, Princess Tea-light races home aboard her mobility scooter, custodian of the stolen plans that can save her people and restore heat to the galaxy....

7.00 THE GAS FACTOR
Simon Cowell, Louis Walsh, *anyone* and a random robot pop star, mount a hostile takeover of British Gas. When customers ring up to complain of poor service, they are greeted with automated messages such as 'You made that bill your own', 'The public will love you because you're the bill next door' and 'I'm sorry, but this is the end of the line for you', before the line goes dead. In the winter months there will be a weekly phone-in, where customers can ring a premium rate phoneline to vote for the pensioner they want to save.

8.00 📽 GOOD BILL HUNTING

Matt Damon is Will - a gifted teen with a troubled past and a history of unruly behaviour, whose ability to solve complex mathematical equations is discovered when a professor pins his British Gas 'How we calculated your bill' to the college notice board as a seemingly impossible challenge to his students. Will's life is transformed, but after several failed therapy sessions with bearded funny man Robin Williams, a despondent Will tweets @AlanisMorrissette the correct equation for irony, before sticking his head in an oven and turning on the gas.

10.50 THE BILL (LATE NIGHT)

(Contains mild swearing and one risqué joke that was funny in 1992.) The popular '90s police drama returns to our screens for a one-off special. June and Reg are called to a disturbance at the 5 million pound mansion of British Gas CEO Sam Laidlaw (nickname: Sammy Two Pools), only to discover that a deranged Mancunian poet has taken him hostage. In a race against time, June must convince the poet not to turn up the mansion's thermostat, which would send British Gas into administration and diminish the value of her shares, while Reg creeps up behind him with Laidlaw's giant butterfly net - still containing the entangled corpses of several endangered species of butterfly. In a tense finale, the poet leaps through a window onto a pile of £500 notes that the CEO has left lying around, then runs home to mock up a vitriolic TV listing, in the hope that he can cathartically dispel some of his hatred for the self-serving, energy-mercenaries who see no shame in calling themselves British Gas, whilst forcing Britain's most vulnerable into fuel poverty.

The Art Business

A networking party for arty types.
Somehow I've been invited
and because I sometimes come over all shy at these things,
I've decided to drink myself confident.

And as it transpires, in under two hours
and just shy of four (seemingly innocuous) pints,
confidence is no longer a problem.

So why is this night proving to be so difficult for me?

Well, it could be four schools' worth of creative cruelty.
It could be the almost definitive damage
done by kids who aspire to be evil office managers.
It could be association.
It could be that on occasion -
even though they've been pinned back for twenty years -
these ears still hear jeers that can dictate social situations.

Or, it could be

that I'm here alone
and that a lot of these people know someone
and have formed small, intimate groups
with their backs to me.

I catch my reflection
and reflect on it.
It looks desperate.
But then
(like an incredibly loud fart
in an incredibly packed lift)
conflict chips in with an unexpected gift:

"Swearing in poetry is just dumbing down the text,"
says a woman I haven't met yet,
in a group that I've approached twice
and felt like Bruce Willis in *The Sixth Sense* both times,
except that I see *ignorant* people.

Isn't it amazing that when your diplomatic reflexes
are dumbed down by wine,
your mouth works just fine.
"What about 'Fuck'?" I hear myself say,
as I crowbar my way into the conversation.
"Is there a better word for 'Fuck' than 'Fuck'?
When you stub your toe, do you say 'By jingo,
I've stubbed my toe!'
Or do you say 'Fuck me, that hurt!'?
Maybe we should use made up swear words
like they did in the '80s.
In those days it was all the rage to overdub swear words
with inoffensive text that was out of context.
They almost always did it in the films
that mum won't like me admitting I watched as a kid
and it never did *me* any 'mothercrushing' harm!"

The alarm on their faces
tells me that even in a conversation
about substitute swear words in the '80s,
crushing mums is still pretty heinous
and this is no place for that kind of language,
thank you very much.
The tuts are resounding,
but the mouthpiece just keeps on grinding out
old cop show classics…

"Forget you, you lousy maggot farmers!!"

I note the way their eyebrows rise

in a kind of synchronised surprise
that epitomises their lack of life lessons.

"What the fax are you looking at?!"

Did I just say that?
Did I just fashion a quip out of office equipment?

"There's always one who lowers the tone,"
says a guy who I know is called Mark, but I choose to call John.
"On the contrary John…" I say.
"My tone is just in stark contrast
to that drone that you've got going on.
My tone soars high above your gap year anecdotes
about goat herding in the Pyrenees,
or that time you were at the same party as John Cleese.
[YAWN]
My tone is leaner, meaner and keener.
If your tone is Princess Di, my tone is Xena.
Compared to your tone, my tone is Tone Loc
(Funky Cold Medina)."
Either someone they really hate just walked in behind me,
or judging by their faces,
putting John in his place has done me no favours.

But *what the fudge*?! Right?
I didn't ask to play this game tonight,
but now it feels like win / win for me:
if you're genuine and don't take yourself too seriously
then we'll get on like a house on fire, or better,
because how much fun can a house fire be?

I'll have made a new friend.

And if you're pretentious…
If you mention pretty much everything you've ever done,

in your opening sentence,
or assume as soon as I enter the room,
that I'm the scally portrait your ignorance just painted,
then I'll just make my excuses
and let you move on
to someone more useful.
But as I'm starting to think that my drink's been spiked
with some kind of truth drug,
I short-change our exchange
and (arms up, palms out) back slowly away,
signalling a truce...

Steady...Steady...
Think it, don't say it...
'Missing you already.'

Now would be a good time to call it a night,
but I find myself ascending the stage
to where the compere left his mic...

"Don't you think..." I *boom out* to the entire room,
"...that in some ways, '80s censorship is similar to this?

Not so much a metaphor, but certain similarities.
They glossed over swear words.
We gloss over vanity.
They embraced thinly veiled insults.
We *embrace* thinly veiled insults.
They invented new ways of saying 'bollocks'.
We invented new ways of *talking* bollocks.
Censorship ages like a cheap wine
and when I'm at these things, I get hints of...
cliques... and... *personal critique,*
box ticks... and... *bullshit.*
Is this it?
Is this what our predecessors fought for?

Is this why those sleepless nights were called for?
Who markets hardest? Who farts loudest?
What happened to word of mouth
and home is where the art is?
Did I really turn up just too late
for the drug-fuelled naked parties?

Idealistic? Maybe. Perhaps a touch naïve.
I *did* take the course on resonating
and not the business degree.
But if you're looking for someone to blame for this rant
then don't point the finger at me.
Isn't it partly my job as a writer
to tell it how it is?
Isn't it partly your job as organisers
to make it less painful than this?
Isn't it partly our job as human beings
not to behave like dicks?

And while we're at it...

If we're calling ourselves artists
then surely we want a career
judged solely on our art
by a jury of our peers.

Because the last time I checked
my looks, my age,
my sexual preference,
my arse-kissing technique,
my adolescence,
my old YouTube footage,
the Mancunian twang when I speak,
my past and present Facebook friends,
the state of my mental health,

my habit of oversharing
and then underselling myself...
had nothing to do with my art at all."

At this point I become aware of the staring.
Like a room full of appalled mannequins -
no-one moves an inch, no-one says anything.
Then I think I see one woman be sick in her purse.

"I'm sorry," I say, edging closer to the Exit.
"It's a hard truth to digest.

Maybe you aren't quite as inclusive
as your funding forms suggest."

"DON'T DO IT.
THEY'LL NEVER KNOW IT WAS YOU."

(The voices)

In early 2014, I hosted a night at Studio Salford.
I had planned to jokingly keep the audience in line with
'The Balls of Shame' -
several tennis balls that I had cut open and placed notes inside.
The notes contained some (quite harsh) criticisms.
The plan being to throw the balls playfully at anyone disrupting the show
and get them to read out the note, thereby insulting themselves.

However, everyone was so well-behaved on the night
that the balls weren't needed.
I packed them all up and went home.

Or so I thought.

To whoever found the one that I left behind -
I hope you didn't take it personally.
I was too embarrassed to tell anyone about it at the time.

Sorry.

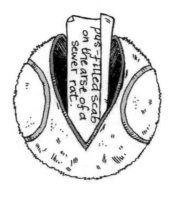

Public Apology No.2

In June 2014, I performed at Green Gathering.
Before I was due to perform, I sat on quiet hillside in the sun,
with a beer and worked on my set.
After a couple of idyllic hours, a wasp decided to crash my party.
I proceeded to do what any self-respecting man would do in that situation:
I ran around in a circle flailing my arms,
then admitted defeat and walked back down the hill.

On my way down the hill, I noticed a woman heading up and
realising that she had witnessed the flailing incident from a distance,
I decided to engage her in conversation.

What I should have said is this… "Wasps eh!"
What I actually said was this… "It's the voices again."

If you are the woman in question -
you walked away too fast for me to tell you I was joking -
you looked distressed.

Sorry.

"ESCAPISM?
YOU MEAN LIKE A MAGICIAN?"

Kaya Farrell
(Insightful 6 year old)

"EXACTLY LIKE A MAGICIAN."

Dave Viney
(Silly Man)

My Mind Is Spider-Man

My mind is Spider-Man.
Could climb skyscrapers,
but takes the less glamorous approach.
Insists the ghost rooms of our boarded up Bingo Hall
are crying out to be imagined.
Says "Clarity begins at home."

My mind is sneak-peeker;
thrill-seeker extraordinaire!
But knows an uncharted supermarket when it sees one -
perches patiently on top
of the staff room vending machine,
unseen and unheard -
laps up every word of an imaginary conversation
between a woman in her forties called Sandra
and an insecure security guard (Tony),
who refuses to guarantee
anyone's safety.

My mind is a dysfunctional Spider-Man.
Knows the day's past saving,
but saves images from motorways
and replays them in pointless dreams
that no dream book explains:
blurred trees, hay bales in bin bags.

Will not spell out my issues in road cones -

says "I'm sorry, but the best I can do
is an emergency telephone
and a cloud shaped like a farmland animal."

My mind's an all-action distraction -

bus surfs the Number 15,
while seated below, a more reserved me
keeps earphones in tight, volume up -
tries to tune out his shouts of

"Oi, boring!!
Get a motorist's attention,
then lick the window."

Get a motorist's attention,
then lick the window?

I don't.
But I want to.

I don't
because a 37 year old sees bacteria
where a boy sees fun.

I don't
because a 37 year old sees consequence
where a boy sees none.

I don't
because my mind is Spider-Man
and despite what 'He' thinks, up there...

Spider-Man does NOT
lick
windows.

You Will Get Out

I'm on a train back from London when I hear it.
Four rows along a woman on her phone says
"Sarah, I promise you…
next time I'm down we *will* get out."
Her words should wash over me -
in no way a threat to me and yet
a tourniquet tightens around my chest.
Heart drums up a protest,
leaving rib cage reverberating with dissident beats
and breath so shallow it catches on teeth.
(Panic played out in Silence)
and though my phone is powerless in my pocket,
I take a call of my own;
an inner voice reassures me
You *will* get out.

Heart appears to have turned the tables -
now somehow able to send messages to Brain:
a twenty-four frames per second account
of a confined life -
penned-in dreams.
A film reel that snags on a familiar scene:

I'm at the same function room party,
in the same run down youth centre,
in the same patched up town,
in the same overpriced round,
watching the same war-painted gran
sing 'Total Eclipse of the Heart'
and all I can think is...

My heart's not in it.

There are adventures that I haven't had yet,
sunsets that I haven't seen yet.
There's a bar on a beach
run by a one-eyed Mexican
with questionable ethics
and I haven't been yet.

"You *will* get out."
Louder this time.
Runs through my mind like the 6 year old me,
who when asked
"And what d'you want to be when you grow up?"
shook his head and said
"Don't wanna be a *grown up!*"

He knew his heart wasn't in it.

There were adventures that he hadn't had yet,
lifelong friends who he hadn't met yet.

"You *will* get out."
Louder still.
The train window vibrates
and for a second I mistakenly think
that I have telekinetic powers…
then the Express rockets past.
Rattles glass like our train is the comedown
and their train is the rush.
Blurred arses pushed up against windows.
Anything goes in Coach D -
the Debauchery Coach.

"You *will* get out."
Loud enough to be heard by other passengers surely.
But then maybe it's not just about me.
What if it's *We*…?

"We *will* get out."
If not by physical means,
then in our minds.
If not in this moment, this day,
this week, this month, this year,
then in our own time...

"We *will* get out."

About an hour or so later, the train's pulling into York
and I'm talking myself out of an overpriced KitKat
when a voice that sounds a lot like mine says
"Scene 21, Take 54, Action!"
(21 - because it's a 21st birthday party;
54 - coincidently the number of pints it would take
to make the 'Macarena' appeal to me).
Action!
Then the *clack* of a clapper board -
cue music and a woman's strained vocal chords,
cue hardmen underpinned by lager and sausage rolls,
cue Extras throwing shapes on a parquet dance floor,
cue DJ who looks suspiciously like
he might play Simply Red.
I don't get caught up in the plotline.
This time I edit instead:

I'm at the same function room party,
in the same run down youth centre
(but it's the run down youth centre
that paid the troubled me attention),
in the same patched up town
(but it's the patched up town
with lifelong friends),
in the same overpriced round
(but it is *still* cheaper than it is Down South),
watching the same war-painted gran

sing 'Total Eclipse of The Heart'
with a sleeve full of hearts
and a heart full of false starts,
gripping that microphone
like her life depends on it
and who knows,
maybe it does.

But this time when her song ends
I stand and clap.
I clap until eyebrows are raised
and jaws are dropped,
until faces soften and my hands begin to ache,
until the Extras feel obliged to join in,
until wolf whistles streak across the room like fireworks,
until her face lights up like Thomas Edison's bank manager,
until this moment, this beautiful moment
is punctured by the opening chords

of Simply Red.

The Plague Of Busy

The car park attendant sits through days singed with sunshine.
More bloke now than lad.
Swapped the Plague of Busy for the Costa del Solitude
and never looked back.

Spends grey-banned afternoons
watching cars become ovens
from a plastic chair that looks like it's seen some action.
Has an internal dialogue -
two plastic chairs in glorious one-upmanship;
random chair: "You don't know you're born!
I spent six years in a comprehensive."
His chair (gravelly American accent):
"See this crack in my plastic...
VIETNAM.
We were winning when I left."

Used to see days through bead curtain rain.
Half-drowned customers with jackets overhead;
Looked like question marks he thought,
but the only answers *he* ever had were 4 across,
Clue: 'without inspiration', 10 letters...
Starts with a 'U'...

_ _ _ _ _ _ _ _ _ _ .
Gets more out of *¡Hola!*
than he ever did from *Hello*.
Knows cerveza tastes infinitely sweeter than beer
and that a lie-in can never compete with a siesta.
Sometimes misses sarcasm.
But wouldn't know quintessentially British now
if it slapped him in the face,
so just misses the word instead:
Quintessential.

Conjures up carnivals in his downtime
where potential Mrs Car Park Attendants
dance through his daydreams,
confetti their enthusiasm
and laugh in high definition -
swapped the Plague of Busy
for the Costa del Solidarity
and never looked back.

His dream-woman drives a soft top, top down Cadillac.
Feels mostly Thelma, sometimes Louise.
Channel flicks past *Corrie* in Spanish
and tuts - some things are sacred!

The car park attendant bides his time:
spare chair inside his hut
polished to a crisp sheen,
freshly laundered polo shirt and jeans.
Practices expressions in a postcard-sized mirror -
aims for somewhere between coy and available.

Kiss My Assets

On the day that my debt dies
I'll rise to a preview of my future highlights
showing on the bedroom TV,
with a montage of carefree versions of me
in slow motion, soft focus revelry.

The carpet will be warm sand between my toes

and in the shower, I'll swear blind that
in a shameless act of symbolism
I saw droplets form pound signs,
before disappearing
down the plug hole.

Downstairs a drum-roll
will herald the return of the *boxy* and *outdated,*
the *just add imagination,*
the *far from all singing, all dancing*
and I'll welcome back my unintentionally retro friends -
it's my Top Ten of *things I put in a safe place*
and never saw again

lined up like ghosts of Christmases past in the living room.

And though debt will be dead to me
I'll still be running for that bus,
because a crust doesn't earn itself
and debt specialises in its own resurrection
and stealth.

But on the day that my debt dies
the bus driver will refuse to take my fare.

He'll just wink and tell me to enjoy the show,
as the side of the bus lifts
like the flap of an envelope
to reveal...

Pensioners and hoodies in a bus queue conga,
a monster-truck flattening the entire British Gas fleet,
a human cannonball, fired
from the top of the multi-storey car park
into a back yard paddling pool on Jackson Street.

Legions of straight-laces, off their faces, letting their hair down,
clearly on the pop, lollipop-twirling lollipop ladies,
tangerine mothers with face-painted babies,
BMX bandits launching fireworks from their handle-bars,
curiously good music from the big bass / small cock turbo cars.

And as the local taggers
put the finishing touches
to the thirty-foot letters of

WELL DONE MATE!

I'll be sending a courtesy text to my boss
to tell him there's a chance I'll be late.

"JUST TELL 'EM IT'S FOOTBALL AND IF THEY HATE IT THAT MUCH, THEY CAN SKIP THE NEXT FOUR PAGES."

Dan Bennett
(Friend, unnecessary pundit, straight talker)

It's the sun coming up and the bets going down.
It's the beer that's bought in and your mates coming round.
It's use it or lose it - no seats reserved.
It's "Get us a can to calm me nerves."
It's never a given and always a game.
It's never nailed on 'cause it's never the same.
It's all over the papers and under your skin.
It's not just the points that you get if you win.
It's bragging and tagging and rubbing it in.
It's giving 'em lip and it's one on the chin.

It's only a game if you don't know the score.
It's never as good as the decade before.
It's thank god that player is ours, not theirs!
It's knowing that *yeah* - he's a spoilt millionaire but
it's knowing he's *our* spoilt millionaire.
It's fans to the rescue with face value tickets.
It's telling the touts by the ground where to stick it.
It's your yearly wage and star player's compared.
It's millions more reasons to hate billionaires.
It's old school, new boots and expensive lessons.
It's sarcastic statements disguised as questions:

"What the fucking hell was that?!"
"What the fuck ing hell was that?!"

It's bad pies and good balls.
It's never played but knows-it-all.
It's biting nails and pre-match tension.
It's shitting the cat up when dad goes mental.
It's sunshine beer garden sing-alongs.
It's righting last year's derby wrongs.
It's 3 points dropped and post match gloom.

It's don't mention the elephant in the room.
It's "Stop Me If You Think You've Heard This One Before."
It's "That Joke Isn't Funny Anymore."
It's "Bigmouth Strikes Again."
It's "Shut it Barry you bell-end!"

It's winning the argument or losing face.
It's coming first in a two horse race.
It's coming *second* in a two horse race.
It's not even being at the races.
It's hitting the bar and our 'cum faces'
(although when I say *our* 'cum faces'
I mean *your* 'cum faces' -
in both cases I usually just curl into a ball and weep).

It's 20% vision / 80% graft.
It's kicking a ball in the park for a laugh.
It's *goalposts* for goalposts - our park's gone upmarket.
It's pie in the SKY TV transfer targets.

It's when you get on that pitch and your day to day,
your nob 'ead boss, your bills to pay,
your grind, your grief, your gritted teeth,
your stress excess, your disarray
gets left behind -
a world away.

It's the new kit on sale (though it looks much the same).
It's the kids want that player they've got on the brain.
It's *must* have his squad number, *must* have his surname.
It's trying to put someone else in the frame.
It's *Please pick the player with the shortest name!*
It's £2.50 a letter, so you try in vain, but
it's vanLongestNameInTheFlamin'World again! and
it's no laughing matter, but

it's a funny old game.

A Game Of Two Scarves

The Panini '84 sticker album -
football stickers trigger a young boy's competitive streak.
Let it be known -
money is for stickers and stickers alone.
Pages 17 and 18 parade red, white and
why can't I get Kevin Moran?
Alan Johnson has Kevin Moran.
Scott Downes has Kevin Moran.
Alan and Scott do NOT have a swap of Kevin Moran.
Dad's a red, but mum's a blue
and maybe that had nothing to do with the divorce.
I was young enough to forget -
happy in my own space cadet.
The kid usually gets custody of the football.

She wore, she wore, she wore a scarlet ribbon.
She wore a scarlet ribbon in the merry month of May

This is common ground.
This is hugging strangers -
be stranger not to.
This is talking to dad as an equal.
Eric thinks in seagulls;
mad as a box of frogs.
But frogs with magic in their boots
and upturned collars.

And when I asked her why she wore that ribbon,
she said it's for United and we're going to Wemb(er)ley

Our dad -
tongue sharp, ready and deadly
from 3 yards of a TV on matchday.

Says the charm's gone out of the game.
"I've got more loyalty on my Tesco's Clubcard," he'll say.
But he still turns up the volume
and he still can't look away.

Tracey Neville's off her head, off her head, off her head.
Tracey Neville's off her head.
She plays netball.

If it's an after-match rush for a pokey pub crush you're after,
then you're in luck mate.
Fate has smiled on you.
You've had your thrills, now get your spills,
You didn't want a full pint anyway,
but wait…

What are we doing here?
Isn't this whole thing just one big metaphor
for male insecurity?
Aren't we secretly yearning for something more meaningful?
No?
Oh right, ok.
In that case I *will* stay for that pint.

Cheers.

"SINCE WHEN DID YOU KNOW ANYTHING?"

Mark Laney
(~~Friend~~ Acquaintance, lousy maggot farmer)

Pre-Poem
(not really a thing)

I don't know much as knowledge goes,
but this I'm sure of, this I know:

Manners are classless.

Affluence is not snobbery.

Snobbery is snobbery.

First impressions
should be the last thing on our minds.

(Oh, and Nibbles is the Noun, not the Verb)

What I Know

Ok, so some opulent function room functions
serve a function,
but this function's function seems to me to be
to make me feel
like my roots are exposed:

Clothes, not the issue;
This suit – cheaper (obviously)
but passable.
Stubble - well it's that safe length
between five o'clock shadow and nine o'clock scally –
happy just to be mingling with the more
distinguished facial fuzz,
but it's not easy to mingle because
this accent is a BIG FAT FLY in their soup
and this fly's bloated, doing backstroke,
having a whale of a time –
shouting "This soup's great mate! What is it?
No, don't tell me, don't tell me, don't tell me…

Heinz!"

We have very different life skills;
They will never agonise over which knife
to use for their Starter.
I can stand by a bar; look half asleep, or lost in thought –
the queue six deep, whilst being ignored
by the bar staff
and still know that that lad in the corner's
itching for a fight;
Eyes tight on his victim, who pushed past him
in the *wrong way*.

I know the right way.
If there is a *right* way.

I know just how much eye contact
shows teenage years punctuated with feet and fists.
My eyes inform his.
This is what I know.

I didn't ask to know this.
It's not so much *I am what I am*,
as *it is what it is*.

Knowing what money really costs
is lost on this crowd;
loud as mouths with unground teeth in;
grins that have never feared bills;
want the thrills of my teenage days,
but not the risk.

I suspect that they suspect that I don't belong here.
I suspect that they expect me to *Doggy-bag* the buffet
and drink all the beer.
And I suspect that I might just do the latter
(as a protest vote!)
But what I know is
that on a good day, I am a good man
and that life is learning, laughter,
live and let live
and after the lesson of today,
I know we will see the same things

but never in the same way.

"POKING FUN AT LOVE, RELATIONSHIPS,
HEARTBREAK - ALL THAT BOLLOCKS -
THAT'S THE HEALTHIEST THING IN THE WORLD."

Mick
(Pub patron and multiple divorcee)

Slow Dance In The Fast Lane

I've tried truth and faith,
but your lies prevail.
You're the final word
of the tallest tale.

I've tried laughter and love,
but you're wound so tight.
You're the black and blue
of a title fight.

I've tried the silent treatment,
but when you talk
you're the finest hour
of the oldest clock.

I've tried breaking up,
but your wrath's renowned.
You're an ancient boyfriend
burial ground.

I've tried keeping my distance,
but when you're near
you're the first cold beer
of a brand new year.

I've tried teasing and games,
but your tongue's so sharp -
you're the win at all costs,
not the taking part.

I've tried making eyes,
but if looks could kill
you're the kung-fu movie
double-bill.

I've tried pulling my weight,
but you give no support.
You're the first I'd pick
as a last resort.

I've tried self-control,
but your words in my ear!
You're my filthiest thoughts
made crystal clear

and I've tried settling down,
but you don't feel the same.
You could have been the first dance at our wedding,
but you're a slow dance in the fast lane.

Prambush

This is no ordinary barbecue.
This is a 'baby ambush'.
It hits me in a series of swelled belly-sized revelations:
we are the only couple *yet to conceive.*

The conversation between those who've
recently removed buns from their ovens
and those whose ovens are still busy baking
turns in graphic detail to the act of giving birth
and I withdraw to my quiet place.

But today it's a burning barricade
of baby buggies and flashing, bleeping
child distraction devices,
and my face is covered protester-style
with a Bob the Builder bib.
It says

Can we fix it? Yes We Can!

(in reference to the catchphrase
that Bob uses to feign enthusiasm,
before turning up late and overcharging)
and as I re-enter reality,
to see her cradling someone's new born,
I think

Can we fix it? Can we fu...

...ndamentally change the way people think
about having babies?

No Bob, we can't.

So leaving her to coo and covet
I make my way to the barbecue,
wondering if there's any way I could carve the words
NOT BARREN, JUST BABYLESS
into a string of sausages.
At the very least
I can work on conceiving a food baby of my own.

She thinks that I'd make a great dad.
I think...
Who'd win in a fight?
A Giant Baby or a Sumo Wrestler?

As soon as I make it to meat
a sympathiser sidles up,
and in a watchyourback whisper
describes witnessing his son's
birth at the business end as like
"Watching your favourite pub burn down!"

"Too much information."

In spite of their cravings
for ice cream on toast
and peanut butter on chips,
the Babe-arian Hordes descend on the barbecue
like ravenous Teletubbies,
bellybuttons protruding like the pointing fingers of babies.
Babies pointing at me, saying *"You...*

Put down the phallic symbol
and step away from the barbecue.
There's salad for people like you!"

I slip silently back into my quiet place.
I sometimes watch films here,

but today the DVD player has cake in it
and the 60 inch, flat screen TV
has this message scrawled across it in strawberry jam...

NOT BARREN, JUST BABYLESS

(PS: It is not seedless jam.)

She was a Thomas-Boy
(not a Tom-Boy -
she took it more seriously than that).
He was hand-me-downtrodden
with the world on his back
and they were postcodes apart,
but he knew her secret -
she kept the key to her heart
under a pixelated plant pot.

They shared dredged up dreams,
lost and found
leftover laughter.
They were out of date -
best before Happy Ever After.
But every evening they had dinner
in a pixelated restaurant.
He bought pixelated flowers.
She would tease him for the gesture
and the world made sense
for those few hours spent online
in a place where the only baggage
was the pixelated kind.

It's Great When You're Eight (Them Mushy Pea Blues)

For a fork full of mushy peas
you let me be your main squeeze.
Yeah, it's great when you're eight,
but girls are so hard to please.

They say love hurts -
ain't that the truth!
You just dumped me with no excuse.
Yeah, it's great when you're eight,
but watch your heart don't get bruised.

We played Hide and Fruitless Seek.
You did all the hiding.
I did all the seeking.
We weren't an item so to speak.
How do you find true love when there's no peeking?

And it wasn't long after that
that you hooked up with my mate Jack.
Yeah, it's great when you're eight,
but you've still gotta watch your back.

Now we're older - those days are gone.
For six lunch breaks you were 'The One'.
Yeah, it's great when you're eight,
but we're nine now and I've moved on.

We played Hide and Fruitless Seek.
You did all the hiding.
I did all the seeking.
We were a Rumour of the Week.
How do you find true love when there's no peeking?

I Avoid You

After Hovis Presley's 'I Rely On You'

I avoid you
like bulls avoid china shops,
like Glaswegians avoid lager tops,
like contented lemmings
avoid sheer drops.

I avoid you
like Paul avoided Yoko,
like a hug avoids a hobo,
like Premiership footballers
avoid a Fiat Punto.

I avoid you
like students avoid a spring clean,
like the dentist avoids a good magazine,
like contagious people in films
avoid quarantine.

I avoid you
like the pissed avoid fruit,
like an egotist avoids a mute,
like people who don't like
[People & Places] or
[Arts & Entertainment] or
[Science & Nature] or
[Sports & Leisure] or
[History]
avoid Trivial Pursuit.

I avoid you
like the late avoid clocks,
like heads avoid chopping blocks,

like sandals should avoid
white socks.

I avoid you
like WAGs avoid a wage,
like Acid House avoided beige,
like The Royal Shakespeare Company
avoids Nicholas Cage.

I avoid you
like a cause avoids a rebel,
like boy-racers avoid treble,
like Neville Neville's parents
should've avoided the name
Neville.

I avoid you
like models avoid snacks,
like porn stars avoid an anti-climax,
like the dad of the world's fattest kid
avoids piggy-backs.

I avoid you.

Cardiovascular

I love you like words:
(the good ones)
like 'hippopotamus'.
Ok, maybe not hippopotamus.
What I mean is you're better than 'Tax'.
This went so much better when I pictured it in my head.

This is a sonnet to the cynical.
It's technically not even a sonnet.
It's a heart shaped box of cyanide chocolates,
but more whimsical because it
HATES consumerism, but likes hugs
and its cynicism comes from a good place -
a place that says
"I love you…

with all my garage flowers!"

It's that after hours, after thought, aftertaste
of hasty confectionary.
It's "You bought a teddy with a heart on it
and you'll have to live with that for the rest of your life man!"
"Don't lecture me!…

…I'm sensitive."

This is a call out to those who'd fall out over nothing,
rather than sit through one more viewing of *Twilight*.
A *Fight Night* on the Scrabble tiles…
"Yeah I know it's in the dictionary,
but it's bit insensitive don't you think?
No? Ok, Fine. If you want PREMATURE
then you can have PREMATURE.
It's completely your call Flappytits!"

This is the tree with the message
"Happy Commercially Orchestrated Romance Day"
carved into the bark,
because actual trees trump recycled cards
and yeah, she might like a balloon shaped like a heart,

but not a pig's heart
from the butchers,
with a bow on it,
because she once told you that she likes the film *Babe*.

This is a sonnet to the cynical.
The clinical removal of the tear glands.
Banned substances include
perfume, massage oils and aftershave.
This is a conviction to P D A -
(Public Displays of Affliction).

It doesn't actually *want* a kiss
and even if you *had* a kiss
it wouldn't *want* it...
unless you were fit or somefink.

Ring a ring of roses
BOOM!
You know there's a mushroom cloud
blooming behind your eyes,
threatening to burst through the top of your head
and destroy this room, but instead...
nothing.
No tables burst into flames.
No flesh is stripped from bone.
No-one sees or feels the words
you just received on your phone.

This is a sonic boom sonnet to the cynical.
The quizzical look that demands
"Tell me something LESS romantic
than a designated day for romance?"

"AH, I THINK I SEE WHAT YOU'VE DONE THERE.
A LITTLE POETRY FOR BIG KIDS IS IT?"

John Hattley
(Friend, big kid, 'Arteest')

My Dad's Bigger Than Your Dad

"My dad's bigger than your dad."
That's what he said when we first met.
Told me his name was Liam and it was raining, he was wet,
so I said he could stand under my umbrella -
said "There's room enough for two under here little fella."
And that's when he said it - this tiny little lad,
he said "My dad's bigger than your dad."

I was shocked so I laughed.
I said "Don't be so daft!
You've never met my dad
and anyway, he's six foot four."
He said "That just might be
but my dad's bigger than yours."

I said "Just how big is this dad?
And don't say bigger than mine."
He said "Bigger than everybody else's dads,
stood on each other's shoulders
at the same time."

I said "What, everyone in Manchester?!"
He said "No, everyone in the WORLD!"
I said "I'm sorry kid, this tale's too tall.
I don't believe a word!"

But still he said *"My dad's bigger than your dad.*
My dad's bigger than your dad.
My dad's bigger than yourrrrrr dad."
He just wouldn't let it go.

So I said "Maybe you should stand under *his* umbrella -
it must be big and perfect for this kind of weather

and I should get going." But then as I said goodbye
tears began forming in the corners of his eyes
and I felt guilty...
'til he pinched his nose between his finger and his thumb
and said "Dad fart! Makes my eyes water -
the gasses from his massive bum.
Just one of the perils of being
a dad that's bigger than your dad's son."

Well that was it! The final straw
and I started to leave, but this almighty roar -
a voice like nothing I'd heard before
stopped me in my tracks. How could I ignore
a woman's voice, so loud it made a passing pigeon cry!?
And I recognised the words that no child can defy...

"Liam!
Your tea's ready!!"

And as Liam turned to run
he said "Love to stay, but I can't be late.

My mum's bigger than your mum."

Billy Big Feet Needs Tea

Billy Big Feet hardly ever goes out.
You wouldn't either if your feet grew a foot
every time you left the house.
But Billy's out of tea bags
and believe me,
if there's one thing a lad with giant feet needs,
it's the calming effect of a good cup of tea.
Although a friend who makes shoes is also pretty important.

So Billy has some thinking to do.
Does he pop out to the shop for tea
and add a foot to his already record-breaking feet,
or stay in and do without his beloved brew?

Billy stays at home.

But all that's on TV
are adverts for PG Tips
and Tetley's Make Teabags...
Make Tea!
And gradually he realises
that he simply can't wait,
so he rings his mate
Timmy Tiny Fingers.

Now, Timmy has tiny fingers, obviously,
and he's been meaning to buy a specially adapted phone,
but not gotten round to it and as he lives alone
he can't take the call.

So Billy tries another friend.
A friend who he's upset before,
a friend he knows won't take much more.

Lisa Long Face.

Lisa answers the phone on the first ring.

Now, you'd never accuse Billy of shape-ism,
but he's always used humour as a coping mechanism
and he can't resist a joke when it's presented to him,
so he asks...
"Why the long face?"

Lisa hangs up.

And from there it goes from bad to worse -
although his circle of friends appear diverse,
one by one - they're all busy or cursed:

Barry Bleak Eyes
is banned from the shop
for depressing the staff.

Jimmy Jangles When He Walks
gets mugged.

Tommy Tall Tales
is on a golfing holiday
in the Caribbean...

with Tiger Woods.

And so, on the plus side,
Billy gets to keep his £1 (and 59 pence),
but on the negative,
he's forced to live a miserable tea-less existence.

Now the moral of this story
(if there's a moral here at all)

is that if you have an unfortunate affliction
and a sizeable tea addiction
and you need someone to call,
first try friends with appropriate names
such as *Tina Time on her Hands,*
or *Benny Big Heart,*
or *Sarah Selfless,*

or Paul.

"I'D NEVER LET IT GET TO ME LIKE THAT. I'D TELL MYSELF TO SNAP OUT OF IT."

More people than you'd think
(Em*pathetic*)

The Condition My Condition Is In (BDD)

In scripted skin that I refuse to shed,
I stumble haphazardly through minefields of information.
Minefields primed to explode at any moment,
sending ideas like shrapnel
(razor sharp, penny-sized epiphanies)
slicing through brain tissue;
synapses shredded like paper -
a nest for open mouthed fledgling thoughts
begging to be fed.

My mind snaps back into place
like shape memory alloy,
grinds against angles like over-familiarity.
I am a monster of my own making
(wrecking-ball anger)
climbing ten storey verses like Kong,
one hand holding my kicking, screaming procrastination,
the other swatting distractions like biplanes.

The future unfolds before my eyes
like a soul searching screensaver:
morphing from a prism into a cube,
from a cube into a sphere,
from a sphere into doubt,
from doubt into hope,
from hope into caution,
from caution into confusion,
from confusion into fear,
from fear into fight,
from fight into...

I no longer find comfort
in the grey bearded face of Wisdom.

I am bound by prophesies penned in invisible ink,
half-truths expanded into bibles,
rituals that rule deposed democracies,
consequences bunched into fists.

This isn't the bullet that penetrated Roosevelt's speech,
but not his heart.
This isn't the bullet that ended Lincoln so theatrically.
It isn't the bomb
that bounced off Franz Ferdinand's motorcade
or the bullet that found his throat less than one hour later.
History will never know this assassination attempt.
No inaugural ceremonies will be held to commemorate
the day that it was thwarted.

From my grassy knoll…
the unmistakable sound of metal on metal;
the slide and lock of a bolt action rifle.

I talk into my sleeve;
step up security.

Shapes

Got my Game Face on.

Got to keep it together - weather the storm,
act normal, no drama.
I *will* take the brunt of the blunt force trauma
that life dishes out, face on.

Because I'm a one step forward, two steps back in time
kind of guy.
A have no faith in fate, but give weight to the paths I take
and the paths that I have taken
kind of guy
and that is why I look for footprints before I take steps,
because there are some footsteps you may regret following in...

Mine are family footsteps that could be the breaking of me -
left me with an inmate's size 10 imprint on my memory
of my father's harsh sentence that predates me,
of my half-brother's sentence that captivates me,
of those out of order inner voices that kept telling me

'I bet you'd make a wicked criminal -
smarter than your average idiot young man.'

I can honestly tell you that I'm not a career criminal,
but I do like the look of their pension plan.

I would be the first to say
that I've been bent out of shape
in oh so many ways,
that I've lost sight of the boy I was,
the joy I had - the lad took over -
sold his soul to the young man

and the young man made plans
that never lasted longer than the day that they were made.

Today that man stands before you - not evolved,
but older and smart enough to know that if he says he's *wiser*
you might just call him on it,
might just 'Once upon a time' him on it.
So instead he tries to *be* 'on it' -
treats every day like a school day,
learns that the best way to avoid sounding like a dick
is to stick to talking in first person.
Makes a mental note to do that in this next verse
and says...

Got my Game Face on.

Got to keep it together - weather the storm,
act normal, no drama.
I *will* take the brunt of the blunt force trauma
that life dishes out, face on.

Because I'm a monkey see,
monkey do not see the point in posturing
kind of guy.
A lost in his own possibilities -
what if these 'why nots',
what if these 'what ifs',
what if these 'when wills',
what if these 'why can'ts'
aren't even the right questions to invest my time in
kind of guy,
and that is why I know less truth now than I did as a child,
because there are some lessons you wish you could unlearn -
wish you could turn back that toy clock,
stop at the moment you realised which shapes
fitted into which holes
and tell yourself "NO!!

Don't do it Little Me!!
Are you just putting pieces in a puzzle,
or will this be your first pigeon-holing?
Your first unknowing exposure
to the closed off thinking that grown ups,
blinkered by their own ambition,
use to put people in their place.

Shapes can change

in the most beautiful, expressive ways.
They can blend, bend and circumvent.
They are not meant to be restrictive."
This heavy shit would of course be wasted
on the very confused Baby You.

Somehow, in the midst of all this,
a wistful ME has managed to sit down and write a list of MEs
that he thinks *might* make it to old age -
a betting slip if you will,
of grey MEs at evens with themselves.
It reads:

ME, ME, ME, ME, ME and ME.

Hands it to ME, it's read by ME who tells ME
"Take a punt on this instead",
points to an image in my head; a poker game
being played in the darkest, coldest corner of my brain:
five MEs,
all with their Game face on,
sat around a poker table -
each unable to read the other
because they're exactly the same,
and so the game looks all set for a stalemate,
when suddenly one ME

changes shape,

breaks into a grin, slams down an unbeatable hand
and demands his winnings, before cashing in
a huge pile of poker chips,
all of which are inscribed with the words

Remember me
and a picture of my Non-Game Face.

"That's it!" the Balanced ME says. "I'm done.
I've got enough here to become

my own man."

"ADMIT IT. SOMETIMES YOU WRITE THE PUN BEFORE THE POEM. TELL THE TRUTH."

Paul Matthews
(Friend, Master of Interrogation)

Dye Hard

BLACK
Black is a vinyl LP
played once, recorded,
taken back.

GREEN
Green is a fussy crocodile,
flossing his teeth
for the human in between.

YELLOW
Yellow is daffodils at a flower show,
before a usually disciplined lawnmower
let itself go.

RED
Red is a sky at night,
wasted on a shepherd
with poor eyesight.

BLUE
Blue is a feeling.
Blue is 'My baby gone and left me',
not 'Dancing On The Ceiling'.

(Red and Blue never follow the rules.)

WHITE
White is chalked words
on a blackboard overnight:
I must not use school books for self-expression.
I must not be allowed to write...

BLACK
Black is berets and combats
in the unlikely documentary
'When Poets Attack!!'

GREEN
Green is leftover side-salad
and its envy of ice-cream.

YELLOW
Yellow is shark infested custard
and a JAWS-inspired cello.

RED
Red is a fast food carton dancing in the wind,
with a newspaper spread that says
Ditch the junk - stay Slim.

BLUE
Blue is the rinse.
Blue is a last ditch hairdo honey-trap
for a silver-haired prince.

(Red and Blue never follow the rules.)

WHITE
White is a whiteboard -
manager's delight...
I must aspire to your pie chart perfection.
I must not be your 'shoot on sight'.

Hello.
Do you find that your mind struggles to comprehend
basic concepts, such as accessing the internet
or opening a cook book?
You do?
Then you're in luck!!
If you've somehow been left in charge of a BT landline,
or managed to find a mobile phone network
for people who've been lobotomised,
then why not call us on 0845 33 I-D-I-O-T.

CALL US...

if you're self-raising flour won't rise to the occasion,
if you're gingerbread man's Caucasian.

SEE WHAT WE DID THERE...

If your cock-a-leekie soup's sprung a leak,
if your family's fasting... EVERY WEEK!!
if your hotpot's not so hot,
if your pasty's nasty,
if your supper's scuppered
and your buns have been shunned,
if no-one has eyes for your steak and kidney pies,

if your dainty pork parcels are returned to sender,
if a peace offering meal signals no surrender,
if your blue cheese sauce is grounds for divorce,
if you think that a grill is part of a fish,
if she thanks you for her Valentine's meal
with a Glasgow Kiss,

IF YOU CAN BURN BEANS!!

CALL US!!

If they've cordoned off your Cordon Bleu,
if there's armed response from restaurateurs;
"Put down the cheesy meaty treat
and come out with your hands up."

If your strawberry cheesecake's just deserts,
if you put A&E on red alert
whenever you turn your oven on,
if friends recommend cooking
at Gas Mark None

CALL US!!

Need your cookery spoon-fed to you?

CALL US!!

0845 33 I-D-I-O-T

We guarantee cooking skills
that WILL lead to a long term relationship.
That promotion you've been after - IT'S YOURS!!
You're mother-in-law will like you
and we mean REALLY LIKE YOU!!

Become a cookery legend in your own lunchtime
for only six thousand pence per minute from a UK landline.*

---

* Calls from people who are considerably more stupid
  will cost considerably more.

"AND FINALLY..."

Dave Viney
(Clairvoyant)

Not since the days of blah blah blah and etc etc, have people cared less about historical accuracy. Huge technological strides have been made in the way we interact with our entertainment. Sitting on a settee (that's right, settees still exist - let's not get carried away), you blink your eyes twice in quick succession and your vision is filled with a televised image:

"Good evening and welcome to News Northwest, I'm Dave Viney.

A teenager appeared at Manchester Crown Court earlier today accused of hacking into his school's computer.

16 year old Aaron Steadman is alleged to have changed his exam results from a B, four Cs and a D, to a Call of Duty 5-Star combat rating. The teenager's mother Mary Steadman says the war-based computer game must take some of the blame for her son's actions.

Character witness, Professor Edward Grimes (formerly of pop abomination Jedward, now Head of English at Oxford University), refused to condemn Steadman, describing him as "Super sick mega totes amazeballs", before leaping around like a chimp in a banana factory.

Steadman himself spoke only to defend his actions with two military themed misquotes: "It's not the winning, it's the taking the other guy apart that counts" and "Imitation is the sincerest form of stealth assassination."

Critics of the Conservative / Jeremy Kyle coalition claim that a possible source of these misquotes and a factor in the overall decline in educational standards can be traced back to August 2017, when the coalition removed all educational material from the internet to make room for an unprecedented growth in social media sites, such as Facebook, Twitter, Twitterbook, Facetwit, BookOfFaces,

Twitface, FaceKindle, Tweetyface, Retweetyface, Bookmyface, TheFaceThatLaunchedaThousandTweets, and of course the award-winning OhGoOnThenShowUsWhatYouHadForYourTea.com.

Minister for Education, Kerry Katona, released this statement in the last hour: "S'pose no-one can be sure of the exact origins of these misquotes. But as the saying goes, 'You can fool some of the people some of the time, but 9 out of 10 cats prefer it when you don't'."

In an unusual turn of events, proceedings were halted when Steadman appeared to make a break for freedom. Wearing a pin-striped, pine coloured suit, the defendant attempted to blend into his surroundings and could be seen inching slowly towards the exit, before being led back to the dock by bemused court officials.

Although a verdict has yet to be reached in the case, Anti-violence in Video Games campaigners are already calling for strict new guidelines.

Working on the principle that all young people are unable to separate gaming from reality, they propose a three tier solution that they maintain will not only stop exposure to violence in video games, but may also solve the world's energy crisis:

Step 1: All computer gaming machines dated after 1982 will be confiscated and destroyed.

Step 2: All persons under the age of 18 will be allocated a 1982 ZX Spectrum home computer with a copy of the '80s classic computer game 'Manic Miner', in which a miner travels through a series of mines jumping over hazardous objects and being generally manic.

Step 3: Upon their 18th birthday, all persons will be sent (willingly) to work in coal mines, in order to ensure the planet has fuel for the foreseeable future.

And finally…

Merseyside's got talent!

Christopher Baines and Salty the Snail of Burton on the Wirral have made it through to the final of *Britain's Got Talent*. They'll go head to head in the final on April 21st with sister act Tongue Twister, who wowed the judges in the semi-final with their ability to construct multiple sentences without using the word 'like' out of context, or the word 'erm'. Well we *like erm* both here at *News Northwest*, so we wish both acts the best of luck.

That's it from me. I'll be back tomorrow with another round up of the regional news and a look forward to the weekend's self-obsessed inevitability.

Take care now."

BONUS FEATURES

RUSHOLME ROULETTE

Dave Viney

The 10 minute play *Rusholme Roulette* was one of 6 chosen
by the BBC for their Turn Up the Talent showcase.

Directed by Helen Varley, it was first performed to an
audience of industry professionals at Media City,
Salford Quays, Gtr Manchester on 20th March 2013.

Cast:

Shaun McGowan:	Brian
Laura Naylor:	Melissa
Stefan Gumbs:	Steve

Directed by Dave Viney, it was also performed for
Studio Salford's Embryo in October 2013.

Cast:

Shaun McGowan:	Brian
Laura Naylor:	Melissa
Clay Whitter:	Steve

SCENE: INT. TAXI – MANCHESTER / RUSHOLME'S CURRY MILE (early hours of the morning).

LIGHTS UP

THERE ARE FOUR CHAIRS ON STAGE. THE FRONT CHAIRS ARE SLIGHTLY LOWER AND REPRESENT THE DRIVER / PASSENGER SEAT OF OUR TAXI. THE TWO HIGHER CHAIRS TO THE REAR REPRESENT THE BACK SEAT.

IN THE DRIVER'S SEAT A MAN, MID TO LATE 40s, READS THE LOCAL PAPER. ONE OF THE ARTICLES APPEARS TO HAVE TICKLED HIM.

BRIAN: (chuckling and shaking his head) Danny, Danny, Danny... We'll be seeing you soon sunshine.

MELISSA (A BUSINESS WOMAN IN HER 30s, WELL DRESSED WITH AN EXPENSIVE LOOKING LEATHER SATCHEL) AND STEVE (LATE 20s / EARLY 30s – 'BAD LAD') ENTER.

THEY OPEN THEIR RESPECTIVE PASSENGER 'DOORS' AND SIT DOWN ON THE REAR CHAIRS AT THE SAME TIME, CLOSING THE 'DOORS'.

THE DRIVER LOWERS HIS PAPER A LITTLE, TAKING AN INTEREST IN HIS PASSENGERS.

MELISSA AND STEVE ADDRESS BRIAN AT THE SAME TIME—

MELISSA: Salford Quays please.   **STEVE:** Dealey Close.

MELISSA: (to Steve, politely) I'm sorry, this is taken.

STEVE: (bluntly) Yeah it is, by me. Dealey Close, near Sevenways mate.

MELISSA: (friendly) Look, I'm sorry. Again. This is my fault. I wasn't clear – it's been a long day. I have a flight in five hours...

MELISSA OPENS HER SATCHEL AND BEGINS TO RUMMAGE.

Here, let me contribute towards another cab...

SHE RETRIEVES HER PURSE AND TAKES OUT A £10 NOTE.

For your inconvenience.

STEVE WAVES AWAY THE MONEY.

STEVE: (irritated) It's always about money with you lot innit! You just assume my day's been a piece of piss and that yours is more important. Well I've got a newsflash for yer Barbie – my day's been shit! And *now* I'd like to go home if that's alright with you.

BRIAN FOLDS HIS PAPER AND ADJUSTS HIS 'REAR VIEW MIRROR' SO THAT HE CAN SEE THEM BOTH.

BRIAN: Ok folks, let's not get over excited. Unfortunately I can't take you both, but...

MELISSA: I'm sure we can come to some sort of compromise. How much would it cost in total? I really am happy to cover the cost of both journeys.

STEVE: (to Melissa) Are you deaf?! I don't—

BRIAN: (interrupting) Total cost, you say? Well, taking into account the cost of road tax, MOT... Then of course you've got tyre replacement, weather's looking a bit dodgy – are you familiar with Bad Weather Tax?

MELISSA AND STEVE DON'T GET THE JOKE.

(jovial) I'm just pulling your leg... *legs*. I was playing on a common misconception, a sweeping generalisation if you like, that all taxi drivers are dishonest in some way.

STEVE: (impatient) That's interesting that, yeah. How much to Dealey Close?

BRIAN: Like I said, I can't take you both or I'll be for the high jump. Although technically speaking it's a low jump...

STEVE: (impatience growing) You on some sort of wind-up you or what?

BRIAN: I don't suppose either of you have got a burning desire for eternal damnation? Sorry, ignore me – just thinking out loud.

STEVE: Look, if you're some sort of god-botherer you're wasting your time mate!

BRIAN: (furious) Eh!! You see a cross hanging from this mirror? No you don't, so mind your fucking manners!

STEVE IS SURPRISED BY THE OUTBURST – UNSURE WHETHER TO RESPOND.
BRIAN TAKES A FEW SECONDS – REGAINS HIS COMPOSURE.

Sorry Stevie... I, er... I get a bit touchy when it comes to rival firms.

STEVE: It's *Steve*. How d'you know my name anyway? We know each other?

BRIAN IGNORES THE QUESTION.
MELISSA HAS HAD ENOUGH. SHE SUBTLY TRIES TO OPEN HER PASSENGER DOOR.

BRIAN: I wouldn't waste your time with that door Melissa – it's locked.

STEVE: Hey! I *said* how d'you know my name?

AGAIN, BRIAN IGNORES THE QUESTION.
MELISSA MAKES ANOTHER ATTEMPT TO OPEN THE DOOR.

MELISSA: Look, I don't know what kind of game you're playing or how you know our names, but you need to let me out of this taxi right now or I'm calling the police.

BRIAN: No can do I'm afraid. Oh and I wouldn't bother with your phone either – no signal.

> MELISSA TAKES HER PHONE OUT OF HER SATCHEL AND TRIES IT. NO SIGNAL.
> STEVE TRIES HIS 'DOOR' AND DISCOVERS THAT IT TOO IS LOCKED. HE IS NOT SO EASILY DETERRED AND TRIES BRUTE FORCE.
> MELISSA HAS NOT GIVEN UP ON HER PHONE – SHE TRIES AGAIN.

I've never had two before. Heard of it yeah, but never two of me own. I have to admit, you knocked me for six. It's supposed to be a slow burner, you know – menacing looks in the rear-view mirror, gradually turning up the heating, sinister hints "How long have you been on mate?" "An *eternity*!" – that kind of thing. But you two completely threw me.

> BRIAN TAKES A PIECE OF PAPER OUT OF HIS POCKET AND UNFOLDS IT.

Now might not be the best time, but as we're breaking all the rules, I have this evaluation form...

> STEVE GIVES UP ON HIS DOOR AND BANGS ON THE 'GLASS PARTITION' SEPARATING PASSENGERS AND DRIVER.

Maybe later.

> BRIAN REFOLDS THE EVALUATION SHEET AND PUTS IT BACK IN HIS POCKET.

STEVE: (angry, worry creeping in) You best let me out of here now! This is kidnap this! 8 years minimum!

BRIAN: You sound like you're talking from experience Stevie.

STEVE: Don't test me mate, I'll smash it!

STEVE BANGS ON THE 'GLASS PARTITION' AGAIN.

BRIAN: That glass is vomit-proof, fire-proof, bullet-proof and muppet-proof, so I wouldn't waste your time if I were you.

MELISSA: Look, if it's money that you want...

BRIAN: You know Mel – can I call you Mel? Is that alright? – as much as it pains me to agree with Stevie, he's got a point – you're like a broken record...

BRIAN BREAKS INTO A RENDITION OF 'MONEY MONEY MONEY' BY ABBA.

Money money money... must be funny... in a rich man's world... Aaaahhh, aaahhhaaaaa...

MELISSA: (raising her voice to be heard above the singing) This is ridiculous! Let me out! **(to Steve)** Try your phone.

STEVE TRIES HIS PHONE.

STEVE: No signal.

BRIAN: Don't mind Stevie, Mel. He's a bit shy round girls, aren't you Stevie. *Money money money, must be funny...*

STEVE: Alright!... Alright. Whatever you want. Just let me out yeah.

BRIAN: The truth.

STEVE: The truth about what?

BRIAN: You *know what* Stevie. Why don't you tell us what happened last week.

MELISSA: What's he talking about? Please, just tell him what he wants to hear.

BRIAN: You too Mel. Don't be shy. Maybe you should get what happened last July off your chest.

MELISSA IS VISIBLY RATTLED.

Oh you didn't think I knew about that? It's very similar to that film *I Know What You Did Last Summer* and the sequel *I Still Know What You Did Last Summer* and the lesser known DVD release *I'll Always Know What You Did Last Summer*.

MELISSA: (darker) You don't know what you're talking about. You know nothing about me.

BRIAN: Oh I know *everything* about you. Knew as soon as you stepped into the cab – perk of the job: Melissa Maycroft (Mel to your friends) – only child – birth mark on your left thigh shaped like Venezuela – favourite food: sushi - recently dumped by fiancé Mark because he wants a lady in the street, but a freak between the sheets. Steven Berry – youngest of three equally unpleasant brothers – single for four years – not by choice – tells his friends his favourite programme is *Babe Station* – favourite programme: *Come Dine With Me* – pet hate: being called *Stevie* – bed-wetter until the age of 12. And that's just me favourite bits.

MELISSA AND STEVE ARE TOO SHOCKED TO RESPOND.
STEVE BREAKS THE SILENCE.

STEVE: This is a blag. There's no way you could know all that. There's a hidden camera in here somewhere. Lee, if this is you you're getting battered!

BRIAN: Come on Stevie! You really think Lee (the Lemon) Sutton and the rest of your plebs could pull this off? If they fell into a barrel of tits they'd come out sucking their thumbs! Think of a number, go on... GO ON!! Sixteen... And another... eighty-four... seven... six hundred and twenty-two. We can do colours if you like... You're trying not to now aren't yer... Ah, there we go... blue... brown... green... yellow... black... Now you see, I would say black's *not* a colour, but you know, tomato / tomATEo... Yellow (again). Come on Stevie, you can do better than this... *Cerise* – just the *word* 'cerise' though, 'cause you don't actually know what colour that is do yer mate.

STEVE IS STRUCK DUMB BY BRIAN'S ABILITY TO READ HIS MIND.

Ok, here's the thing... We're short on time and if I'm honest, I've made a right bollock of building the tension and terror, so I'll get straight to the point... Unfortunately, you're going to Hell. *Actual* Hell. Not Middlesbrough. I get that all the time. Hell is a lot hotter. It usually works like this... Punter gets in, I turn the meter on, then it's off to Hell, via Gorton. I might put 'Highway to Hell' on the stereo, I might not. You can over-egg it, you know? Anyway, usually the longer it takes to confess - the higher the level of eternal pain and anguish - The Boss's big on people taking pride in their evil. Problem is there's two of you and I can only take one... So, unless anyone's got any better ideas, it looks like we're down to *'One Potater, Two Potater'*.

MELISSA IS PROCESSING THE QUICK-FIRE INFORMATION.
STEVE HAS HIS HEAD IN HIS HANDS.

You alright there Stevie mate? You're looking a bit peaky.

STEVE: (subdued) Sometimes I... I get these voices...

BRIAN: *UH-URRR!!* Wrong answer! Try again! We *are* the voices Stevie, and we said *FUCK ALL!!*

STEVE: (aggressive) That's what you wanna hear though right? You freak! I tell my brothers about this and you're a dead man. Open the fucking door, NOW!

BRIAN: (adopts parody Geordie / *Big Brother* accent) Day 1 in Beelzebub's Cab. Stevie is in a bad mood. Melissa is working on a plan to exit the cab. Who goes? You decide.

MELISSA: (mildly flirtatious) Listen, you should let me go. Look at him – he's not sorry. He'll *never* be sorry. I'm intelligent – I can at least *learn* to be a better person.

STEVE: Shut up you stupid cow! *You don't know me!* **(to Brian)** *She* can't have your legs broken. *I* can.

MELISSA: If you let me go now, I swear I will do something decent with my life.

BRIAN: You should take note Stevie-boy – this is how it's done. Continue Melissa, please... This is *very* interesting!

MELISSA: I have money – I could help people.

BRIAN: Go on...

MELISSA: (turning up the flirtation) I'm a woman – I understand compassion. This job must be hard. I could help you relax, soothe your—

BRIAN: (interrupting) *One potater, two potater, three potater, four... Five potater, six potater, seven potater, more...*

BRIAN TURNS AND WAGS HIS FINGER IN SYNC WITH THE RHYME - STEVE, THEN MELISSA, THEN STEVE, THEN MELISSA, THEN STEVE, THEN MELISSA, THEN STEVE...

My... mum... says... it... must... be... you.

BRIAN HAS CHOSEN STEVE. BUT IS IT TO STAY OR TO GO?

Go on then... ...GET OUT NOB 'EAD!!

STEVE CLEARLY CAN'T BELIEVE HIS LUCK. HE QUICKLY OPENS THE
'DOOR' AND GETS OUT.
THE DOOR AUTOMATICALLY SLAMS SHUT BEHIND HIM.
STEVE TRIES THE OUTSIDE DOOR HANDLE – IT'S LOCKED.
HE LOOKS IN AT MELISSA...

STEVE: (to Melissa) It's locked.

STEVE STARTS TO BACK AWAY, THEN TURNS AND RUNS.
[EXIT STAGE LEFT]

BRIAN: No-one likes a creep Melissa.

MELISSA: (cold / true colours) Do you think this scares me? You,
this – it's hilarious. You think this is the first time that I've been
turned over? Just name your price and get it over with you sad,
pathetic little cunt.

BRIAN IGNORES MELISSA AND USES HIS 'RADIO' TO CONTACT
'BASE'.

BRIAN: 54 to Base... Janine, I'm gonna need a high impact fatality
for a Steven Berry – ID.7624298SB. Bus oughta do it. Or a lorry if
there's one nearby. Thanks love. 54 out.

FOR A FEW MOMENTS THERE IS SILENCE IN THE CAB AS BRIAN
SEEMS TO BE WAITING FOR SOMETHING, THEN THE
SCREECHING OF TYRES NEARBY, FOLLOWED BY A LOUD THUD
AND A DISTRESSED FEMALE SCREAM.
BRIAN LOOKS SATISFIED. HE LOOKS AT MELISSA IN HIS REAR
VIEW MIRROR...

Sorry Mel. You were saying?

LIGHTS OUT

END

Hard Time

A song that I wrote for The Reliants in 2007

Lately I'm walking and hoping I'm winning
and winging my way to your door
and I see that it's not the same colour
and wonder if you've changed?
Hasn't it all?

Back to the future - I'm seeing that faces
are making bad names like before,
but I see that they're not the same faces.
Lost in the old ways.
Isn't it all?

> *It's hard (time)*
> *It won't take you back*
> *'til there's no time*
> *to take it all back, so I...*

sit at a bus stop and watch as the cars pass
and maybe a face I recall
will be pressed up against a car window
as they go by smiling.
Shouldn't we all?

Lose all direction and end up in shelters
that kept us from climbing the walls,
back when Pat lost the plot;
Mickey talking a lot, but no action.
Didn't we all?

> *It's hard (time)*
> *It won't take you back*
> *'til there's no time*
> *to take it all back, so I...*

walk back to our road. I know it's not our road,
but still I knock on every door,
just to tell them that we lived and loved here.
If we could relive it,
wouldn't we all?